PUBLIC SPEAKER SECRETS

52 Proven Ways
to Increase Your Impact
Every Time You Speak

Dr. Michael A. Hudson

PUBLIC SPEAKER SECRETS:
52 Proven Ways to Increase Your Impact Every Time You Speak

© 2016 by Dr. Michael A. Hudson. All rights reserved.

No part of this book may be reproduced in any written, electronic, recording, or photocopying form without written permission of the author, Dr. Michael A. Hudson, or the publisher, BooksInPrint.com, CreateSpace Independent Publishing Platform

Published by: CreateSpace Independent Publishing Platform - BooksInPrint.com

Cover & Interior Design: Sel Book Design Service

Editor: Brenda Hudson

ISBN: 978-1-5353133-7-7

First Edition

Printed by BooksInPrint.com - CreateSpace Independent Publishing Platform

DEDICATION

To my grandmother who always encouraged me to speak up and who listened patiently for hours as a young boy searched for his voice while sitting on her couch.

To my father who showed me how to engage with an audience and respond to even the most difficult question with compassion and confidence.

To my mother who believed in me, drove me to every 4-H demonstration contest, and helped me lug all those bulky materials for my demonstrations across the fairgrounds.

To the students, entrepreneurs, small business owners, executives, government agencies and leaders, and many others who were in the audiences where I discovered the secrets shared in this book.

To a man named John Jimenez who spoke at my school when I was in 2nd grade and changed my life by revealing the power of story to engage a distracted kid and focus his attention for the first time while showing him what he could do with his voice.

To my amazing and always supportive wife, Brenda, who FINALLY succeeded in pushing me to share this material in book form, then shepherded the project using that magic that only she possesses for getting stuff done.

TABLE OF CONTENTS

Introduction 1

Speaker Secret #1: Use All Available Resources 4

Speaker Secret #2: Craft Your Messages 7

Speaker Secret #3: Keep It Simple 11

Speaker Secret #4: Use "Tell, Tell, Tell" 14

Speaker Secret #5: Lookout for Listening Styles 17

Speaker Secret #6: Simple Sound Bites Work 21

Speaker Secret #7: Always Arrive Early 24

Speaker Secret #8: Dress for Impact 27

Speaker Secret #9: Check All Equipment 31

Speaker Secret #10: Act as the Leader 35

Speaker Secret #11: Eat for Success 38

Speaker Secret #12: Stay Hydrated.......................... 42

Speaker Secret #13: Manage your Nerves 46

Speaker Secret #14: Connect with Your Audience 50

Speaker Secret #15: Set Up the Room for Success 54

Speaker Secret #16: Work the Microphone..................... 57

Speaker Secret #17: It Starts With the Introduction..... 61

Speaker Secret #18: Don't Speak Too Soon 65

Speaker Secret #19: Open With Impact............................ 68

Speaker Secret #20: Manage Your Time 72

Speaker Secret #21: Just Be Yourself.................................. 76

Speaker Secret #22: Forget the Podium........................... 79

Speaker Secret #23: Stage Positioning.............................. 82

Speaker Secret #24: Stage Memory 86

Speaker Secret #25: Use Humor Effectively.................... 90

Speaker Secret #26: The Power of Threes........................ 93

Speaker Secret #27: Eye Contact Counts......................... 96

Speaker Secret #28: Use Visuals You Can't Touch 99

Speaker Secret #29: Using Computer Visuals 102

Speaker Secret #30: Using A Flip Chart 106

Speaker Secret #31: Managing Your Notes 109

Speaker Secret #32: Using Handouts 112

Speaker Secret #33: Using Gestures 117

Speaker Secret #34: Careful Quotes Increase Impact 120

Speaker Secret #35: Technology Realities 123

Speaker Secret #36: A Caution About Microphones ... 126

Speaker Secret #37: Tracking Your Stories 129

Speaker Secret #38: Don't Be the Hero 132

Speaker Secret #39: Rehearse, Rehearse, Rehearse ... 135

Speaker Secret #40: Vocal Power 139

Speaker Secret #41: The Power In the Pause 142

Speaker Secret #42: Eliminate Ums, Ahs, and Redundant Phrases 146

Speaker Secret #43: Powerful Posture 149

Speaker Secret #44: Engaging Your Audience 152

Speaker Secret #45: Stage Movement 155

Speaker Secret #46: Record Everything 159

Speaker Secret #47: Ending Your Speech..........................162

Speaker Secret #48: Always End On Time......................165

Speaker Secret #49: Close With Impact...........................168

Speaker Secret #50: Thank People Properly 171

Speaker Secret #51: Handling the Q&A 174

Speaker Secret #52: Always Leave Late..........................179

About The Author 182

How to Contact Michael 184

INTRODUCTION

I started my first business when I was just seven years old...riding my bicycle from house to house selling greeting cards and holiday gifts.

Since then I've started a handful of businesses, been a professor in the Big Ten and the Ivy League, and become a trusted advisor to the over 3,000 companies where I've helped them improve service, increase sales, and isolate opportunities for growth.

The material in this book has evolved over the course of more than 30 years, during which I have delivered over 8,000 presentations to audiences including college students, entrepreneurs, small business owners, corporate executives, and board members.

Like most of my projects this one has been a collaborative effort in many ways, some of them a bit unusual.

Public Speaker Secrets

It all started many years ago with the people who pushed me to move beyond my fear of speaking in public—they taught me the foundations that underlie many of the concepts shared in this program.

It continued during my years as a college professor where the pressures of teaching as many as five different courses every semester forced me to get better in all of the areas of presenting that are covered here.

From there, speaking at conventions and delivering on-site programs for growing business clients helped me to discover, test, and refine the ideas shared herein.

My experiences with those presentations, combined with coaching students and executives who wanted to improve their presentation skills, led me to identify the 52 specific actionable ideas.

Each is intended to be practical, easy to implement, and will improve your effectiveness as a presenter, no matter what the situation.

It is my hope that you will find the process of learning this material interesting and that you will put it to good use to achieve the results you desire as you share your ideas in various settings.

Introduction

IT'S YOUR TURN...

Here's how you can get the most impact from this information:

1. Read each *Speaker Secret* and consider how it would impact your success if you applied it.

2. Pause when you finish that specific *Speaker Secret* and take a few minutes to respond to the *It's Your Turn* question with an eye on how you will use it in your next presentation.

3. Keep the book handy as a reference and use it to continuously improve your presentations and increase your impact every time you speak!

SPEAKER SECRET #1

Use All Available Resources

One of the main causes of poor presentations is, frankly, laziness.

What could potentially be a stellar presentation gets derailed because the speaker neglects to use all the resources available to them. They rely too heavily on what they think they already know, and they don't take advantage of simple steps that could greatly enhance their presentation.

Here are some examples of simple things you can do before your presentations to give yourself the best chance for success:

- Do some quick online research that can reinforce key points

Use All Available Resources

- Talk with others who have done this kind of speaking before
- Engage with members of the audience to better understand what they want for the program
- Talk with the meeting planner

Another idea that provides immeasurable benefit is to invite some people to watch a video of you actually delivering a message to an audience, or give them an audio version and ask them to listen to it. Get their feedback. Then take action on their ideas.

Sometimes all you need is a fresh set of eyes and ears to take your message to the next level.

Finally, after you have given that next presentation, be as objective as possible and evaluate how well you did.

Do the work, before you step in front of the room.

Dedicate yourself to learning, honing, and fine-tuning your craft.

Do everything you can to use all available resources.

That is Step One in getting on the path to delivering powerful presentations.

Public Speaker Secrets

IT'S YOUR TURN...

How do you see this tip applying to your presentations?

_____

_____

_____

_____

_____

SPEAKER SECRET #2

Craft Your Messages

The most important preparation step is crafting your message.

You need to begin with the end in mind by asking yourself this question: "What is my real objective?"

- Are you there to persuade the audience to do something?
- Are you there to teach the audience something?
- Are you there to share information with the audience that they need to know because of something they have coming up in their lives?

Whatever you are going to be speaking to the audience about should dictate both the way you deliver your presentation and the way you structure the content for your presentation.

Connect with your audience.

The easiest way to get started with that is to use this as an opportunity to connect with your audience.

Find a way to speak with several audience members prior to the presentation. Spend a few minutes on the phone. Ask them what they expect, what they need, what they want, and what will best serve them from your being in front of their organization. Then take the information they give you and use it to help shape the message you are going to deliver.

Let's consider an example.

Suppose you talked to several audience members who said there was a divide within their organization on how people saw the issue you were coming to talk about. That would tell you immediately that what you need to do to help them the most is give them the two different perspectives that exist on that issue.

As you craft your speech, you want to make sure that you have enough points to cover one alternative, and a matching number of points to cover the other. That way, when you speak to the group, you have done your job. You have informed them about the two alternative perspectives and you allow them to make the decision.

You would do something similar if you were trying to persuade the group to take a specific position. In that case, you would bring the evidence that you have to bear on the situation, share your examples, and help them understand why that makes the case for or against whatever the decision happens to be.

Craft Your Messages

No matter what you do, talking to your audience is a key step in making sure your presentations are a success. If you can find out what they want to hear and then give them what they want to hear, you're going to be more successful.

Remember the real objective of your presentation. Is it to persuade? Teach? Share information? Your objective will dictate the way you deliver your presentation, and the way you structure your content.

Public Speaker Secrets

IT'S YOUR TURN...

So when you're crafting your message, ask yourself this question:

How do I prepare to ensure that my presentation connects with this audience?

_____

_____

_____

_____

_____

SPEAKER SECRET #3

Keep It Simple

Simplicity works.

One of the most important things to keep in mind when crafting your presentation is that simplicity works.

Here is a little personal story.

The reality is that I've struggled with this most of my life, particularly when I first began speaking.

Because my mind is always filled with ideas I tend to think that my job in front of the room is to share all of the ideas I have and allow the audience to make up their minds as to which points are relevant to them.

The truth is that nothing could be further from the truth.

The audience didn't come there to do work; they came there for you to tell them what they need to do or know.

Public Speaker Secrets

That's why your message needs to be kept simple and focused, and why it needs a central theme that can be easily understood.

The point of overcoming audience distraction is really kind of the key here.

Keeping it simple helps your message connect with the audience that already has a lot on their mind.

Here's why simplicity works.

The human mind can handle seven, plus or minus two, pieces of information at any point in time. Think about that. That's between five and nine things that your mind can actually process at any given point.

If, while I'm making my presentation, you are worried about what's for dinner, what you have to pick up on the way home, making sure the kids get home from school safely and where you're going for vacation next month, then I only have five opportunities left to fill any piece of your mind with my information.

That's why we talk about designing all presentations around two to three main points.

Two to three is all it takes to sell most ideas and to effectively present information to an audience so they can comprehend it. If you go longer than that, they're not going to remember it and they're not going to feel your impact.

The key is to stick to two or three. The audience will be able to take that information away and use it because your presentation will be much more memorable.

Keep It Simple

IT'S YOUR TURN...

What are the 2-3 main points in your presentation that you want your audience to remember?

_____

_____

_____

_____

SPEAKER SECRET #4

Use "Tell, Tell, Tell"

The next important concept to consider in crafting your message is the "tell, tell, tell" concept.

1. You begin by telling people what you're going to tell them. That's the opening of your speech.
2. Then you tell them. That's the body of your speech.
3. Then you tell them what you have told them. That's the summary or conclusion of your speech.

Using this very simple "tell, tell, tell" technique will ensure that all of your presentations have impact.

Why?

Because the audience knows what's coming and they can anticipate it. They can listen carefully to see what you are actually saying. At the end, you reinforce the key highlights of your message so they know what the takeaways are.

Use "Tell, Tell, Tell"

Tell people what you're going to say, tell them what you're saying, and tell them what you just told them. Develop your ideas to lead your audience, deliver your core message, and reinforce it by circling back to connect the dots.

"Tell, tell, tell" is alive and kicking.

I know that there's an emerging school of thought that this no longer works, but I strongly disagree.

All one needs to do is watch one of the pseudo news shows on TV to realize that the concept of "tell, tell, tell" is alive and kicking.

They tease the audience with what's coming, they go away, they come back and tease again, at some point they actually deliver, and in the end they recap.

The argument that I've heard against this recently is that you'll lose the younger generation when you do this because they have short attention spans.

My view is that argument actually reinforces why this needs to be done. If you don't keep telling them what it's about and tell them what's coming, they're going to stop listening.

I also think this is a key step in making sure the audience understands what they're going to get out of your presentation so that there's no mystery.

"Tell, tell, tell" is amazingly powerful, incredibly simple, and something you need to learn to do if you're going to craft effective presentations.

Public Speaker Secrets

IT'S YOUR TURN...

How can "tell, tell, tell" help you effectively communicate your message?

_____

_____

_____

_____

_____

SPEAKER SECRET #5

Lookout for Listening Styles

When crafting your message, a very important thing to consider is how people learn. There are visual learners, auditory learners and kinesthetic learners.

Many speakers don't understand that the members of their audience don't all receive your message in the same way.

Visual learners think in pictures. They need you to tell them stories that help them develop a mental picture of what you are talking about.

Visual learners need to see things like:

- PowerPoint slides
- Pictures
- Infographics

Public Speaker Secrets

Show them things that allow them to visualize what you are talking about. They are looking for you to say things like "How things look" and "How you see it" because that connects with the way they listen. About 75% of your listeners will be of this type.

The next group of audience members you will encounter are the auditory learners. Auditory learners, about 20% of our population, are people who listen and hear rather than process by sight.

These are people who want you to be talking about how things sound, what they hear, what they are listening to. They want to hear those words because that connects to them at the auditory level.

These are people who are very comfortable when you read information to them because that helps the auditory part of their brain process the message that you are giving.

For this group, it's okay to read a visual off a slide on a screen. The previous group, the visuals, prefers you not to read it. They would rather read it themselves.

The final type of audience member you encounter is the kinesthetic learners. These are the people who feel things. They want to connect on an emotional level. It's a matter of how things feel to them when they hear you tell your message.

They often have very poor eye contact and will not be very responsive when you are looking at them or asking them for head nods or various verbal attends to let you know they're listening. What they're doing is processing and thinking about how what you are saying makes them feel.

This is only about 5% of the population, but it's a very important 5%. They tend to think in a deeper manner that sometimes reveals some very interesting things about the message you're delivering.

What do you do with these three styles? When you structure your presentation, think about all three styles.

Make sure you have some visual images that will tackle the visual people in the audience and bring them in with you.

Make sure you tell stories that have an auditory component, or that you read some quotes or information off a screen so that the auditory people feel connected.

Make sure you find a way to get the kinesthetic people connected. Talk about how you feel about the information that you're sharing. Ask people how they feel about the information. Consider a hands-on activity where they actually engage in writing down the information and what they think about it. That way, it connects the feeling side of the brain.

Remember, there are visual listeners, auditory listeners, and kinesthetic (feeling) listeners in your audience.

IT'S YOUR TURN...

What types of media can you use to reach the visual learner?

_____

_____

_____

_____

Could you find a way to vary your voice or tell vivid stories to reach the auditory learner?

_____

_____

_____

_____

How can you use emotion to connect with your kinesthetic audience member?

_____

_____

_____

_____

SPEAKER SECRET #6

Simple Sound Bites Work

One of the things that make a presentation incredibly powerful is when you incorporate soundbites that get repeated throughout the presentation.

Brief, focused statements reinforce your core message. These allow the audience to pick up on them and take them home.

This point is all about memorability— how do you make the people remember the key stuff that you want them to take away when they leave your presentation?

It's also about engaging the audience with your message. Using sound bites that you come back to multiple times in a presentation significantly strengthens the impact of your message, equips them to easily share it, and supports them taking action because they have

Public Speaker Secrets

a quick hook that reminds them what you were telling them to do.

Sound bites also create a way to pull the audience in key times during speech.

For example, I once saw a speech where the gentleman was talking about sales techniques. He told a story, and in the context of the story he had a tagline. He came back to that line three different times as he went through his speech.

The next day everyone who was in the audience was talking about the way he used that phrase.

That's the power of a soundbite. It's one of the reasons we see soundbites used so much in our news. They give the listener a very tangible, easy takeaway that they can use moving forward.

Incorporate sound bites or taglines throughout your presentation to reinforce your core message. Repeat these throughout your talk and you'll find audience members reciting it long after your presentation.

Simple SoundBites Work

IT'S YOUR TURN...

What parts of your message could be turned into a memorable sound bite?

_____

_____

_____

_____

SPEAKER SECRET #7

Always Arrive Early

Nothing may be more important to you when giving a speech than arriving early. We've all seen the speaker who dashes in the door at the last minute. The technology doesn't work, the room isn't set up the way they thought it would be, the handouts aren't there and everything just falls apart.

I don't want that to happen to you. My recommendation is to always arrive 45 to 60 minutes before you are scheduled to speak.

Trust, but verify. Check the room out and make sure the layout is the way you want it. Make sure the temperature is where you want it.

Test and re-test all the equipment.

You need to make sure everything works for you. You may have a very competent support staff and the venue, including the sound guy who says, "I checked everything

Always Arrive Early

and it works fine", but following this motto will save you a lot of trouble...trust, but verify everything.

Arriving early also gives you the chance to show your genuine interest in the event. You get a chance to do some meeting and greeting. You get a chance to make the meeting planner feel at ease. Most of all, you get a chance to help yourself relax because you are onsite and not stressed. That is going to make your presentation much, much better. It has been my experience that most people show up too late. It always amazes me how anyone thinks they can walk into a room five minutes before they are going to speak and deliver an effective presentation.

The real message here is that you must take responsibility for what you're going to do and whether or not it's going to succeed when you agree to step in front of any room or stand up and speak in any situation. Frankly, that requires some reconnaissance beforehand. That's why I recommend arriving early and doing the kinds of things that are suggested here.

You can't afford to be caught off-guard by strolling in late. Arrive at least 45 minutes before you speak and set yourself up for success.

IT'S YOUR TURN...

What steps do you need to take to make sure you arrive at your presentation at least 45 minutes early?

_____

_____

_____

_____

_____

SPEAKER SECRET #8

Dress for Impact

There are several different ideas out there about how you should dress when presenting your message.

This particular subject seems to be evolving on a regular basis.

- Do I wear all black so the audience focuses on my message and not my clothes?
- Should I dress in what makes me feel comfortable?
- Does my audience even care what I wear?

The general rule of thumb is to always dress one step above your audience. If your audience is dressed casually, go to the corporate casual level. If your audience is dressed more corporately, then take yourself up one more notch toward an evening out level.

Public Speaker Secrets

You are doing this for two reasons:

1. This gives you a way to connect with your audience so they see you as the authority. You have positioned yourself differently by the way you are dressed.

2. Perhaps more importantly, we all behave differently when we're dressed differently. By being among the best-dressed people in the room, knowing that people are looking at you will change the way you interact with them. It will enhance the effectiveness of your presentation.

Dress one step up above the audience. If the audience will be dressed casually, go corporate casual. If they are dressed corporately, go to an evening out level. This positions you as an authority.

The context of your presentation, the nature of the audience, as well as, the location, need to be considered.

But perhaps the most important point is to ask the person who is bringing you in how they want you dressed. Not only does that connect you better with them, but it gives you more clarity and ensures that you will not make a huge mistake.

Don't gloss over that last point I just made.

When it comes to the way I dress for a presentation, the only person whose opinion really matters is the person who hired me.

People drop the ball here all the time.

It's good to have your own "signature style", but ultimately I want to be a working speaker, and if my style clashes with the event hosts desires I'm not going to get a chance to speak as often as I would like.

Public Speaker Secrets

IT'S YOUR TURN...

What could you change about the way you dress that might increase the impact of your message?

_____

_____

_____

_____

_____

SPEAKER SECRET #9

Check All Equipment

This Speaker Secret makes our list because I've experienced it far too many times.

For example, I've walked into a room where I've been assured that all the equipment and connections were tested. Then I'll hook up my equipment only to discover that it doesn't work.

I've then had to go head-to-head with people who don't even understand technology who insisted it was supposed to work and blame it all on my equipment.

Not only is this unnerving, it is also a horrible way to build an effective relationship with the on-site people, and it threatens to make you look bad in front of the people who hired you.

Even worse, any distraction takes attention off your message.

Let's get specific.

Once you're in the room getting ready for your speech, one of the most important things you can do is to check all the equipment. We mentioned that earlier, but let's get really specific.

1. Make sure all the settings on your computer or laptop are set so that the machine doesn't go to sleep halfway through your presentation. Nothing is more distracting. Take it from personal experience. Nothing is harder to figure out than when your laptop suddenly turns blank and your visuals disappear.

2. Check the microphone. Make sure you know where the on/off switch is and that it's adjusted to a sound level that fits your voice and the way you speak, not someone else's. (It might be worth adding a special point here about microphone batteries which should be brand-new at the start of any presentation and changed mid-day if you're doing an all-day session.)

3. Check the lighting in the room. Who's in charge of the lighting? Who's going to turn the lights up or down?

Notoriously, people who run meetings will think that you need to turn the lights off that are shining on the audience. If you are the speaker and you are trying to connect with the audience, you have to be able to see them. You want to make sure those lights are always

Check All Equipment

turned on so the audience is very visible to you from wherever you are speaking.

The other thing about lighting is to make sure the lights that are shining in the area of the screen or any visuals you're using are set appropriately. If you're using computer projections, you want those lights dim so that the visuals show up well. If you're using some other sort of visual, you may want lights brightened and shined directly on them so that they will perform correctly.

Take that extra five minutes to walk through those three checks and you will be much more effective in using technology to make your presentations strong.

Remember…trust, but verify.

IT'S YOUR TURN...

What steps do you take before your presentation to make sure your equipment is working properly?

_____

_____

_____

_____

_____

SPEAKER SECRET #10

Act as the Leader

Own the room.

One of the challenges anyone faces when speaking to an audience is owning the room.

The simple fact is that when you agree to step on the stage, you are agreeing to care for that audience and protect them. That means if something goes wrong, you take charge because you're the one with the microphone.

You're the one that the audience will be looking to for guidance.

A fire alarm or emergency situation is not the time to look around and wonder to whom you should hand the microphone, it is time to step up and take charge.

This is something that very few speakers ever consider.

Public Speaker Secrets

When you're the speaker, the people in the room are looking to you as their leader, at least for the period of time that you're up there speaking. It's your responsibility if something goes wrong to help those people know what to do.

If, for example, a fire alarm goes off and everyone hears it, they will look to you as the speaker for direction on where to go and how to get there safely.

One of the first things you want to do when you are checking out the room is find out where the fire exits are so that in the event of an alarm, you know where to send people.

You also want to find out if there are any unusual things that may be going on in the area, such as any type of construction or maintenance...anything that can create unnatural noises that the audience would hear and wonder, "What was that? What does it mean to us?"

Remember, you are the speaker. You are in charge of the room. People will look to you for guidance should something out of the ordinary happen. It's your job to make sure you're ready to deal with that.

Act as the Leader

IT'S YOUR TURN...

If an emergency takes place while you're speaking, are you going to be ready to own the room?

_____

_____

_____

_____

_____

SPEAKER SECRET #11

Eat for Success

Eat to have energy.

This one might be a little uncomfortable. I want to take a couple of minutes to talk about how you should eat before you speak.

Early on I made this mistake on a regular basis, indulging in the sometimes rich meals that were being served to the audience before standing up to speak, only to find that the heavy food had adverse effects on my energy, and sometimes my voice.

Obviously, you need to eat to have energy. The best way to do that is to have a little salad with a light dressing and some sort of protein with the salad. That will give you good energy to keep you going through your speech.

Avoid, at all costs, those pre-planned meals that have a lot of rich, creamy gravy and dressings. The high-carb meals are going to slow you down and bring your energy down. Not only that, they're also going to give you some phlegm production in your nasal area and throat. That's going to really destroy your ability to keep your voice strong for a long period of time.

Even if you are only speaking for 15 to 20 minutes, if you're speaking right after a heavy meal, it will show. Eat light, eat carefully and eat cautiously. You can have the cheesecake after your speech, not before.

Drink beverages that will lubricate your throat such as decaffeinated coffee, decaffeinated tea, or water. It's your choice whether it's ice water or room temperature. Some people say that they speak much better with room temperature water. I know others who are just as happy drinking ice cold water. That's your call.

If you're uncomfortable about declining your hosts offer of food, there are multiple options you can use:

- Explain to them that you've already eaten, thank them, and invest your time walking around getting to know the audience.

- Share that you're on a special diet or have special dietary restrictions.

- Let your host know that you have a pre-speaking routine that doesn't include meals, and you want to be in a position to offer them your very best.

Public Speaker Secrets

Above all, avoid all the sweets and heavy foods that will bog you down and lead you to have energy peaks and valleys throughout any lengthy presentation.

Remember to keep the food and beverages light.

You'll be much more prepared to work with your audience and deliver an effective presentation.

IT'S YOUR TURN...

What types of things to you like to eat/avoid before you give a presentation?

_____

_____

_____

_____

_____

SPEAKER SECRET #12

Stay Hydrated

We live in a world where everyone knows that hydration matters, but nothing is worse than being thirsty, and I mean genuinely thirsty, when you're standing in front of room people.

I've been there, I've done that, and it is not a good feeling.

Should that happen, the solution is easy…simply ask someone to please bring you some water. There is always an eager audience member willing to help out, and it's much better to solve the problem than it is to try to bluff your way through it and pretend it doesn't exist.

Also, there is a reality here that may feel a bit uncomfortable, but you don't have to worry about the bathroom issues that may surface in your mind if you think about drinking a lot of water before you walk up step on stage. The truth is your body will process it very

Stay Hydrated

quickly and it will leave you in other ways. Your throat needs to be lubricated and you need to recognize that a lot of water is being expelled invisibly every time you open your mouth to speak.

Our bodies will lose as much as a pint of water during a 30-minute speech. Think about that. If you're doing a two or three-hour presentation, that's an awful lot of water that your body is losing. It needs to be replaced somehow.

There is a debate among some speakers as to whether you should drink water or a beverage with or without ice in it before you speak.

To some degree this is a personal choice, but I can attest to the fact that water with no ice has helped me in many situations, even times when I've had a sore throat and still needed to go on stage.

I'll share an embarrassing story to illustrate my point about the importance of hydration.

I was making a presentation in front of a very important audience that could have led to the securing of a major business contract when my throat dried up and felt like it was going to seal completely shut. It was uncomfortable. There was no water in sight, and it almost cost me a major piece of business. In fact, the only reason it didn't is because I always carry a bottle of water in my briefcase which I keep near me when I'm speaking, so I was able to reach down and grab it, take a sip, and then move forward.

Public Speaker Secrets

You can also ask Marco Rubio who had to awkwardly fumble for a bottle of water on national television while giving his political party's response to the State of the Union speech.

If you're going to be giving a speech that lasts more than 15 to 20 minutes, the most important thing you need to do to take care of yourself is stay hydrated.

Find a non-caffeinated beverage or just plain water, whatever you prefer, and make sure to drink it regularly during your presentation so you keep your hydration level up. That is the key to keeping your energy strong and delivering your powerful message.

I can't stress that enough.

Stay Hydrated

IT'S YOUR TURN...

Do you have any tips on staying hydrated during a presentation?

_____

_____

_____

_____

_____

SPEAKER SECRET #13

Manage your Nerves

It's a fact...everybody gets nervous before they speak. Even the most highly paid, highly established, well-known professionals.

If you talk to them right before they step on the stage, they will tell you that they get nervous. Let's accept the fact that it is a reality and talk about how we deal with it.

Three quick tips.

I'm going to give you three quick tips you can use to deal with your nervousness. They all work, and I still use them to this day. They're easy to adapt, simple to apply, and they will make an impact.

1. Put your hands together and lay them softly in your lap. Not a high-pressure squeeze, just a gentle touch. Take your right thumb press against the palm of your left hand very gently.

Manage your Nerves

There actually is a physiological thing going on here. There is a point in the middle of this palm called the ulnar point which is closest to your heart via the circulatory system. Massaging it relaxes you and calms your nerves.

2. You can also dissipate nervous energy by gently rolling up on the balls of your feet, then returning your heels to the floor and lifting your toes off the floor. It works best when sitting, but it works standing as well. You can simply rise up on the balls of your feet, and then drop back on your heels. You will get the same basic effect.

3. When you are introduced, make sure you get up with confidence, walk to the place you will be speaking and take control of the room before you say anything.

Most of us get nervous about how to actually start our speech while walking up to the podium. You've probably seen people who start too soon. The room isn't even ready for them to talk yet. That is the nervousness kicking in.

Take control of that nervousness by taking control of the room first, and then begin your speech.

Remember, your speech is a conversation with several people at the same time. They do not know what you are going to say, only you do, so you don't need to worry about a misstep or saying the wrong thing. When you do, it makes you feel nervous and that makes you

Public Speaker Secrets

more likely to make mistakes. Just relax, be yourself, and think of the speech as a conversation with several friends as if you were at a party or around a campfire.

If you use these tips, you will find that nerves become a thing of the past for you. You will have much more effectiveness and comfort when you get in front of the room.

IT'S YOUR TURN…

What are some techniques that you use to control your nerves before you speak?

_____

_____

_____

_____

_____

SPEAKER SECRET #14

Connect with Your Audience

Your audience wants you to succeed.

Back in the days when I was petrified of speaking in public, connecting with my audience was my number one fear. I thought the audience was there to judge me; that they would simply be reviewing and critiquing everything I said, and it intimidated me.

Then one day someone pointed out that the audience wants you to succeed because they've invested their time listening to you, and they empathize with your situation. They are actually rooting for you to win.

That changed my perspective, and lead me to realize that if you remember that the audience wants you to succeed, then your job is to connect with them and share a message they want to hear. All concern disappears.

Connect with Your Audience

If you know you have a group of people in the room who are pulling for you, wouldn't it make sense to connect with them before you ever get in front of them?

The answer is yes.

Connect with your audience when they get in the room. Act like you're the host of the meeting, not just the guest speaker.

Walk around, introduce yourself to everyone, give them your name, ask for their name, and ask them what they do. Let them know you are their speaker today. Tell them you're pleased that they came, and you look forward to sharing some time with them. Just establish some casual rapport.

You will build some fans in the audience. They will be the people you can look to because you have already spoken to them. They will give you the head nods that make you feel more confident that what you are saying is being received.

If you're a true celebrity speaker this is probably less important because they already know who you are, but if you're someone whom they've never met, shaking a few hands will go a long way to increasing your chances of success.

An important side note on this topic, since I'm encouraging the shaking of hands, it's important to be prepared and carry some sort of hand sanitizer with you so that after you've shaken all those hands you can remove any germs you may have picked up before you engage in your presentation.

Public Speaker Secrets

I also wipe down all equipment that has been set up that I'll have to touch just as a safety measure.

I know it sounds a little over the top, but I can assure you that it has prevented me from getting sick a lot more than I did before I started doing it, so I highly recommend it.

Remember:

- Connect with your audience when they get in the room.
- Act like you're the host of the meeting, not just the guest speaker.
- Walk around, introduce yourself to everyone, give them your name, ask for their name, and ask them what they do.

It's worth every minute of your time that you spend shaking a few hands, saying hello and thanking people for coming because that builds your base of fans in the audience...fans who want you to succeed. It makes your job that much easier.

IT'S YOUR TURN...

What are some things you do to connect with your audience?

_____

_____

_____

_____

_____

SPEAKER SECRET #15

Set Up the Room for Success

Here is a little-known, seldom-discussed fact. It is the responsibility of the presenter to determine the setup of the room in which they will present.

Think about it.

You're coming into a room to deliver a presentation. Shouldn't you take control of how it is set up to maximize the effectiveness of your presentation?

The answer is absolutely yes.

So what do you do?

Take the time to talk with the meeting planner about how you want the room set up. Give them a diagram. Personally connect with the people who will set up the room to make sure it's set up the way you want.

Set Up the Room for Success

I once walked into a room that was set up completely the opposite of what I had requested.

I shared a diagram in advance, I talked with the meeting planner who hired me, and I talked with the people on site. But somehow when it came time to set up the room all of the fruit of those conversations apparently disappeared, because the room was completely wrong.

Because I showed up almost an hour early to prepare, I was able to immediately identify the problem, but, when I tried to find someone to fix it, no one was available because it was lunchtime and the staff was on break.

So I ran up to my room, quickly changed into casual clothes, came back downstairs and reset the entire room in about 15 minutes by myself. I then went back to my room, got suited up, and came back down and delivered my speech.

Room setup has more impact on presentations than we realize, and the wrong room setup can ruin the best presentation.

Public Speaker Secrets

IT'S YOUR TURN...

What suggestions do you have for successfully setting up a room?

_____

_____

_____

_____

_____

SPEAKER SECRET #16

Work the Microphone

It never ceases to amaze me how many people are scared of the microphone.

My feelings about microphones are probably pretty obvious at this point, but in my opinion you should always use one. End of story.

If there are more than 25 people in the audience, insist on a microphone. You want to make sure the audience gets the message the way you deliver it and the way you want them to receive it.

The role of 25 stated here is a good one follow, but the ambient noise in the setting is equally, if not more, important.

In some situations, you may actually need a microphone for only 10 to 12 people.

For example, one day I was on a training program for salespeople who worked in a factory, and the soundproofing in the training room was marginal at best.

It was very difficult for anyone standing more than five or six feet away to hear me, so a microphone was necessary even though the audience was only 12 people.

Another tip is that if you're not comfortable with the microphone you need to get comfortable either by speaking into your phone and recording yourself or by picking up a toy microphone and just practicing in front of a mirror.

The microphone is your friend, and it helps your message be heard which is a must for an effective presentation.

If you're going to speak in front of groups of 25 or more people, you need to become very comfortable using a microphone. It's not that difficult. It can either clip on to you or you can hold it.

Your comfort level with that microphone is what assures that everyone in your audience hears the message you're delivering.

Ambient noise, bad hearing and simply the way your voice carries in a room all effect the impact of your presentation. Using a microphone ensures that everyone walks out with the message you wanted them to get.

One quick tip about microphones, and a caution: Never tap on a microphone to see whether it's working.

Work the Microphone

It's not good for the microphone and it runs the risk of popping loud noises that are very uncomfortable for the audience.

If you want to test the microphone, simply pick it up and say, "Testing one, two, three. Testing one, two, three." The other benefit this gives you is you get a chance to hear how the microphone puts your voice out into the room.

After all, that's its purpose.

Public Speaker Secrets

IT'S YOUR TURN...

What suggestions do you have about the most effective way to use a microphone?

_____

_____

_____

_____

_____

SPEAKER SECRET #17

It Starts With the Introduction

One of the keys to delivering a powerful speech is a great introduction.

There are two things that you can do to make your introduction great.

1. Get rid of all the background that has nothing to do with why you're speaking to this audience at this time.

They don't care where you went to college, who you dated, what softball team you played on, or how many awards you've won. They care about why you're the person to deliver this message to them today.

That's what your introduction should focus on. It should get the audience's attention. Get them to wonder who the speaker is, then present your name. All of this needs to happen in 30 to 45 seconds at the most.

2. Write your own introduction. Set it up the way you want it read. Print it in a nice, big 18-point font. Put it on a single sheet of paper.

Contact the person who will introduce you. Give it to them. Make sure you teach them the single most important thing you need them to do. When they end your introduction, they turn, welcome you to the stage and begin a hearty round of applause.

Nothing makes you feel more bulletproof when you walk up on stage than an audience that has just applauded for you.

On the flipside, nothing can derail a great presentation as quickly as a bad introduction.

I was once introduced by someone who made reference to having known me since I was "running around pooping in my diapers"...not exactly an auspicious way to walk upon the stage.

In fact, even though I was very confident and well-prepared for my speech, I was thrown off by this rather ridiculous, and in my opinion offensive, introduction.

That's why I feel so strongly about this point...it's up to you to control your introduction, and you need to put in the effort necessary to make sure it is presented correctly. I would go so far as to contact the person who will be introducing me and asking them to actually read the introduction to you beforehand.

It Starts With the Introduction

I know that may sound controlling, but the reality is you want them to read through this at least once, probably multiple times, so they can do it correctly.

When you make this request, make it clear that you need their help to make sure your presentation has the impact they want, and let them know that you've created the introduction to set the stage for your presentation, and you would like them to read it exactly as it is written. Most people will do it. After all they want a successful presentation as much as you do.

If you'll do the two things listed above, and make sure you take control of the introduction process, you'll see much more power out of your speeches.

Public Speaker Secrets

IT'S YOUR TURN...

What's the strangest introduction you've ever been given?

_____

_____

_____

_____

_____

SPEAKER SECRET #18

Don't Speak Too Soon

Have you ever been in a room where someone began their speech and no one was listening?

Or in the place where someone was fighting to get the attention of the people in the room because the room had not yet settled.

This is often going to happen for one reason or another. Sometimes the audience you're speaking to know each other too well and are still engaged in casual conversation, but the person who's in charge of the meeting chooses to introduce you to get things moving forward. At other times people will be eating and are preoccupied in little side conversations.

But here's the reality, if you don't get their attention it's not their fault, it's yours.

You simply have to learn to take command of the room and wait to speak until people are listening.

Public Speaker Secrets

You don't need to cajole them or embarrass them in any way to get them to settle down. Simply take your position on the stage to make your presence known.

Here are some effective keys things to do to begin your presentation:

- Take the stage after your introduction.
- Walk up to where you'll be speaking.
- Stand still.
- Look at the audience, and look around the audience.
- This builds anticipation, and the room is yours.
- Then begin your speech.

You've put your heart and soul into your message, don't let your audience miss a word because you started too soon and they aren't paying attention.

IT'S YOUR TURN...

What is the most effective way you've found to get the attention of your audience?

_____

_____

_____

_____

_____

SPEAKER SECRET #19

Open With Impact

Nothing is more important than how you open the speech.

You're in front of the room. You've taken control.

It's time for you to bring your audience along on the ride that could change their life, and a powerful opening will leave them no choice but to follow you.

There are three basic ways to open a good speech:

1. Tell a story that lets people in on what you think about the subject. It sets the stage for where you're going in your presentation and brings them into your inner circle.

2. Ask a question. Not some meaningless, arbitrary question where you ask the audience to raise their hands and call it audience involvement.

    Ask a question that really probes the core of the subject you're there to talk about...a question that makes them think. It's a question that draws out their viewpoints on it so they're prepared to hear what you have to say.

3. Make a statement. You'll sometimes see this used by people who deal with confrontational issues. They choose to make a statement that they know everyone will disagree with.

It makes everyone suddenly turn around and pay attention to what they're saying. Then they get the chance to share their perspective. The speaker may or may not actually disagree with the audience. They're using it as a trick to get the audience to come to them.

The bottom line is that the way you open a speech in the first 30 seconds or so, will often dictate how well people listen throughout, and how much of your message they actually take with them.

I can't leave this subject about how to take the stage and open your speech without sharing one thing that you should never say or do at the podium.

Never look at your audience and say, "Good morning," and then when they don't respond say, "Well, that was pretty weak! Good morning," and expect them to respond again.

There is nothing that turns an audience off more.

Think about it. You've immediately told them you think they're idiots because they didn't respond. You've turned them off. You've tuned them out.

Public Speaker Secrets

Just because you've seen it done a hundred times doesn't make it right.

Please avoid that at all costs. It doesn't work and it can offend the audience very, very quickly.

If they're offended, they're not listening. If they're not listening, you're not having an impact on them.

IT'S YOUR TURN...

What is the best opening to a speech that you've ever heard?

_____

_____

_____

_____

_____

SPEAKER SECRET #20

Manage Your Time

When you are invited to speak at an event it's your responsibility to figure out what information is most important for you to share in the period of time that you have been given.

It is vitally important that you end on time, regardless of whether you started on time or not.

I can't tell you how many times I've been in situations where I wasn't the first speaker of the day and somewhere along the line somebody was introduced late and went on longer than they should have because they wanted to get their full time.

As a result, I was the speaker who had to clean up and shorten my presentation in order to get the audience out of the room at the promised time.

The point being, it's not fair to the audience, it's not fair to other speakers, and frankly it's not fair to you.

Manage Your Time

Be professional enough to make sure that your speech fits the time available.

I should note here that even though I've often been able to build a very good rapport with my audiences, even in the best circumstances people are still annoyed if you keep them slightly longer than they envisioned being with you.

That's even true if you ask for their permission to share just one more point or give one more clarification.

People's minds are conditioned when they walk into a room to hear a speech regarding how long they will be there based on what has been shared with them.

It's also worth remembering that college and high school classes are scheduled to end 10 minutes early to give people a chance to get to the next event.

So the message of ending on time and managing your time is really important.

Here's one other thing you should never say. "If I had more time, I'd tell you more."

Duh! Anybody would tell you more if they had more time.

Think about the last time you heard a speaker say exactly that. Think about how it made you feel. You felt like they weren't giving you the good stuff. You felt like they didn't really prepare.

The audience knows your time is limited.

Public Speaker Secrets

You know your time is limited.

Why repeat that?

Here is a good rule of thumb...always be the speaker who has a reputation of starting on time and leaving the audience wanting more.

Manage Your Time

IT'S YOUR TURN...

What are your best tips for managing your time during a presentation?

_____

_____

_____

_____

_____

SPEAKER SECRET #21

Just Be Yourself

I've seen good speakers, bad speakers, and great speakers.

The thing that most separates the greats from others is that they are genuine, and authentic, when they are in front of the room.

That's why I recommend that you be yourself when you speak. Nothing is more important.

Trying to be someone else, unless you're doing a role play of a certain character, is not effective. The audience wants to see the real you.

They want to know that the person whose hand they shake prior to that presentation and the person they talk to afterwards is the same person who gave the presentation.

I have seen marginal speakers go a long way by bringing their authenticity to the platform. You can do the same thing…just be you.

If you're a person who normally talks in simple, short sentences, then deliver your speech in simple, short sentences.

If you're a person who tells detailed stories to your friends, then when you craft your speeches, fill them with detailed stories.

One of the best ways to ensure you are being yourself is to rehearse in front of the mirror.

I think it's also important to note that even bad speakers can have a good connection with the audience if they're being real.

People can tell when you are just regurgitating facts and figures.

If you want to develop a genuine connection to your audience, share your story, your observations, and your insights. Bring you to the message.

Focus far more about whether your authentic self is shining through than whether your message is being received.

If you're coming through, the message will always come through.

Public Speaker Secrets

IT'S YOUR TURN...

What are some ways that you have used to connect with your audience?

_____

_____

_____

_____

_____

SPEAKER SECRET #22

Forget the Podium

Have you ever experienced a boring speaker who stands at the podium holding onto it as though it's going to run away, or the person who reads from their notes and never looks up at the audience?

Those speeches are boring because a podium is an artificial boundary between you and the audience. It makes you uncomfortable, and it makes your audience uncomfortable.

Yes, there are times when the content you are sharing has to be factually correct and accurate, and you may need to go to the podium and read, but that doesn't mean you don't pause periodically and look up at the audience to connect with them.

In my humble but accurate opinion, those are the only times you should ever stand behind a podium.

Public Speaker Secrets

Get out among the audience so you can engage with them. Being in their midst will significantly elevate the impact of every presentation. You are eliminating the artificial boundary and becoming one of them.

Granted, it's not feasible to get among the audience in big groups, but you can get out from behind the podium so that your engagement with them is at a different level.

If you have a key point you need to refer to for accuracy, then keep the podium somewhere where you can go to it to check the information, and then step away.

For the most part, a podium gives you reasons to do things you shouldn't, like hang onto it for dear life and fidget with your notes. If you can't move the podium out of the way, step around to the side of it and give your speech from there. If you're in one of those scenarios where there is a dais with a podium and you're expected to speak from up there, be the different speaker.

Walk down from the dais. Stand amongst the crowd and talk with the people.

Be yourself...don't let that podium create an artificial boundary that you have to look and work over.

Your most effective presentations always happen when you are out there connecting with the people.

Forget the Podium

IT'S YOUR TURN...

Are you a speaker who hides behind the podium? What are some things you could do differently to engage your audience?

_____

_____

_____

_____

SPEAKER SECRET #23

Stage Positioning

One of the marks of a great speaker is how they connect with their audience.

What I've discovered in my years of successfully presenting ideas to varied groups is that it's a good idea to have simple, memorable cues to ensure that you are giving your audience the best chance to receive your ideas.

To that end, I developed the Diamond Method.

Think of the area you're speaking in on stage as a big diamond on the floor, or if it helps, imagine the infield of a baseball stadium.

There are five points to that diamond:

1. The front point – Home Plate
2. The back point – Second Base
3. The left point – First Base

Stage Positioning

4. The right point – Third Base

5. The center point – Pitcher's Mound

Put yourself in the role of the pitcher – standing on the mound facing home plate, with the audience in the stands.

You'll have the most impact if you give the majority of your presentation from this center point.

If you want to address a point with your audience by bringing them in close and making a personal connection, you can take a step or two forward, as though you were moving toward home plate. After you've made your point you can return to your center point and continue with your speech.

Suppose you need to address a point with your audience that you know is going to cause them to be a little bit standoffish or uncomfortable...simply step back to the rear (toward second base in our baseball analogy).

By stepping to the rear you put more distance between you and the audience. This makes everyone more comfortable as you address the more delicate points. Again, when you're finished with that point, move back to the center (pitcher's mound).

You can do the same thing by moving to the left or right (first and third bases). This is a great tool to show opposing viewpoints on the same subject. Use the center point (pitcher's mound) as a neutral area. Or, if you have three perspectives on a topic you can use the left, right, and center points to convey them equally.

Public Speaker Secrets

Using the Diamond Method is a stellar way to connect with your audience and help them process the ideas you are presenting.

But there is another powerful way to utilize the Diamond Method that we'll cover in our next Speaker Secret.

For now, keep this diamond in mind because it allows you to use purposeful movement to make your speeches achieve their greatest impact, while creating a close connection with every member of your audience.

IT'S YOUR TURN...

How could you use the Diamond Method to better connect with your audience?

_____

_____

_____

_____

SPEAKER SECRET #24

Stage Memory

In Speaker Secret #23, I introduced you to the Diamond Method and how it could be used as a practical tool to connect with your audience. I'm excited to show you another way you can use the Diamond Method to help you commit your speech to memory and deliver it with maximum impact.

If your speech has three or four main stories or points (and that's about as many points as you can effectively deliver), you can use the Diamond Method to help you easily recall the content of your speech as you deliver it.

1. Start by delivering your opening from the center point on the stage (The Pitcher's Mound) - This will serve as your neutral zone for the speech and is the center of the diamond. You'll link your opening and closing points to this location, and use it as a place to return and set up each of your main points.

Stage Memory

2. Transition into your first key point and bring the audience in by stepping forward (Home Plate) – This first point in the diamond serves as the link to your first key point or story. When you've delivered that point, move back to the center point as you put that story into its proper context and then continue your speech.

3. For your second point, theme or story, move to the left (First Base) - This gives you a chance not only to trigger your memory for the next point, but also to engage with that side of the room. Once you finish that point, return to your center point, and set up your next main point or story.

4. As you deliver your third main point or story, move to the right (Third Base) – Share your story and make your point, connect with that side of the room, then return to your center point and continue.

5. When it's time to wrap up, move back from your center point (Second Base) - Begin your conclusion, then step forward to close your speech by almost going out into the audience. You can also use the back point of the diamond to tackle difficult information or invite the audience to mentally step back if you need to at any point during the presentation.

Public Speaker Secrets

By incorporating this simple diamond into your speech, you create a unique memory technique as you link your key points and stories to the points on the diamond.

Practicing your speech this way in advance will establish a pattern in your mind so you are ready when it's time to deliver in front of the audience.

One important caveat: The size of the 'stage' where you are speaking will determine how many steps you'll take when you move from point to point on the diamond. The general rule of thumb is to move slightly farther than you might feel natural whenever you can.

IT'S YOUR TURN...

Do you ever get lost when giving a presentation? Give the Diamond Method a try and see if it helps you stay on track.

_____

_____

_____

_____

SPEAKER SECRET #25

Use Humor Effectively

Have you ever told a joke that just didn't work?

Trying to tell jokes is dangerous. Chances are you weren't brought to the stage to be a comedian.

I've had jokes fall flat because I didn't recognize the differences in regional humor...sharing something that gets a great laugh in one area of the country and falls flat in another.

I don't have a great deal of international experience, so I can't talk about that dimension, but I know that it could also be problematic.

The simple message is this, if you're naturally funny, or sarcastic, then being genuine on stage demands that you bring that with you. But unless you earn your living as a standup comedian, your job is not to step up in front of the room and tell jokes.

Use Humor Effectively

Humor has to fit the message, and your humor has to be appropriate for the audience. That's not something that comes easy. It requires a great deal of practice, rehearsal, and preparation.

Think about some of the great comedians, speakers, and entertainers. By sharing their personal real-life stories that others can relate to, they connected with their audiences and had a much bigger impact.

That's how humor should fit within your presentations... it is revealed through the stories of life that reveal the day-to-day moments that make us laugh.

So remember rule number one, never tell a joke unless it fits your message perfectly. Real, personal, day-in-the-life stories will always have more impact.

Bring that into your speech, not those same old canned jokes that seldom work.

Public Speaker Secrets

IT'S YOUR TURN...

What was the last story you told that got everyone laughing?

_____

_____

_____

_____

_____

SPEAKER SECRET #26

The Power of Threes

If you have three key themes and each merits three sub points, then use that approach and leverage the power of threes to make it more memorable. And it will help keep it organized inside your mind as well as in the minds of your audience.

***Listen closely.

I'm about to tell you the three most important things to do whenever you give a speech.

Drum roll please...

1. Give three examples
2. Give three examples
3. Give three examples

See what I did there?

Public Speaker Secrets

The quickest path to give a lot of information to people in a manner that they will be able to remember, process, and understand is to leverage the power of threes.

By breaking your message down into three important components, three sub messages, or three core themes, you will connect with the audience in a way that's memorable, and it gives you an easy way to format your speech.

If you can use alliteration within the threes, that's even better. Or, if you like to use acronyms or acrostics that works well also.

In addition, using sub points under each of the main points (surprise surprise...three of them under each) allows you to make nine key points in a focused presentation.

If you have one key theme, offer three pieces of evidence or three stories.

If you have three key themes then offer one story, example, or one piece of evidence for each.

There is magic in using three examples, three key points, or three illustrations.

People's minds can capture it easily and it gives you an ability to show different perspectives.

It's also a nice thinking and recollection tool, both for you and your audience.

When you learn to use the power of threes you'll have an easy way to manage your message while exponentially increasing the effectiveness of your presentations.

IT'S YOUR TURN...

What are three ways you could use the Power of Threes to enhance your next presentation?

_____

_____

_____

_____

SPEAKER SECRET #27

Eye Contact Counts

Nothing has more impact in your speaking than your ability to make eye contact with the members of your audience.

When your eyes meet theirs in the midst of a point and you hold that connection, you get a chance for a lot of things to happen.

- They understand that you're focused on them and paying attention to how they are reacting to what you're sharing.

- You get a chance to see what they think with a head nod, a smile or something they communicate to you with their eyes that lets you know that they indeed are getting the message.

I recognize that there are those of you who are uncomfortable with this, and don't do it very well naturally. That said, it is important to note that the most

Eye Contact Counts

effective speakers always make eye contact with their audience.

Here is an effective tool I use that will help. As you're working through your speech, make eye contact with an individual and count silently to yourself 1...2...3... and then move to the next person. That makes the eye contact long enough to be impactful, but not so long that it becomes uncomfortable. It's also equally effective to look at a person until you make a complete point and then move onto the next person.

Here are the three biggest benefits to making eye contact:

1. It creates personal connection
2. It makes people feel special
3. It makes you look real

It also takes your speaking to another level. You're no longer one of those people who simply scans the room looking for friendly faces. You actually make direct, one-on-one connections.

Try this. I guarantee you'll see the difference.

Public Speaker Secrets

IT'S YOUR TURN...

Do you trust people that are unwilling to look you in the eye?

_____

_____

_____

_____

_____

SPEAKER SECRET #28

Use Visuals You Can't Touch

Few things have more impact in a presentation than great visuals. Unfortunately, many people use them incorrectly.

The power of story creates a mental picture with the audience.

Imagine an attorney making his case before a jury. He has them close their eyes as he uses his words to paint a picture that transports them to a particular time and place. This tactic allows him to guide them to see what he wants them to see, and it's an incredibly powerful illustration of the power of story and its ability to create visuals that you cannot touch.

You may have a tremendous visual presentation that accompanies your speech, but what happens if the A/V isn't working properly?

Most speakers would be dead in the water.

That's why it's always a good idea to practice your speech with, and without the visual component. The serendipity of doing this is that you'll learn to move the audience emotionally and that will increase their connection with you, the memorability of your presentation, and the impact you have.

If you can tell the story in a vivid manner with a lot of descriptions and details, you will actually paint a picture in the minds of your listeners. They come right along with you on the journey. That makes it a lot easier to take them where you want them to go.

If you can learn to use stories, you'll become a masterful speaker very, very quickly. You'll find yourself not only in demand, but also increasing your impact on every audience that you speak to.

Stories have power.

Stories are magical.

When you give a presentation, share them and watch what happens.

IT'S YOUR TURN...

Think of a story that has moved you personally. What was it about the story that affected you? Can you see the power of using vivid stories in your presentation?

_____

_____

_____

_____

SPEAKER SECRET #29

Using Computer Visuals

One of the greatest inventions of all time for speakers is computer generated visuals.

Yes, I'm talking about Microsoft PowerPoint and other tools like:

- Keynote
- Haiku Deck
- Prezi
- Slideshare

And the countless other fantastic tools that exist.

Aside from being an effective way to reinforce your message on the screen, they are also a great way to build your list by offering to share your slides with the audience if they provide you with an email address.

Using Computer Visuals

These tools are an effective way to reinforce your message on the screen by delivering salient points and bringing home your ideas to the audience.

The challenge with these tools is that too many people use them incorrectly. They put all the information they want to talk about on the slide, turn to the screen and read it to their audience. This has become an accepted practice in our field, but the problem is that it doesn't work. If your entire presentation is in the visuals, then what do they need you for? Your visuals are there to support your speech, not give it for you.

Here are some simple, quick rules you can use to make your visual presentations more effective:

1. Never use more than three to five points per slide. That will keep them at the right size and the right level so people throughout the audience can read them. It keeps that slide focused on a common theme.

2. Never have more than five to seven words in any one of those bullets.

3. Always make sure that you use graphics whenever possible on your slides. Graphics convey a lot more information a lot more quickly than words.

Another option is Guy Kawasaki's 10-20-30 rule...

- No more than 10 slides in a presentation
- No more than 20 words on the slide
- No Font smaller than 30 point

Public Speaker Secrets

Whether you're using pie charts, bar graphs, photos, or clip, the bottom line is very simple; Craft your slides to support your presentation. Don't allow them to become your presentation. You are your presentation. Your visuals are there to reinforce your message.

IT'S YOUR TURN...

Have you ever been guilty of reading your presentation off your slides? Would you consider that speech a success?

_____

_____

_____

_____

_____

SPEAKER SECRET #30

Using A Flip Chart

One of the more powerful, but often overlooked tools for bringing visuals into your presentation is a simple flipchart.

In today's technology heavy world, people tend to think that there is no value in writing things on a flipchart. But nothing could be further from the truth.

In reality, the audience feels more engaged when they see their words and ideas appear in front of them, and there's not a great way to do this without using a flipchart. It's worth practicing on the flip chart so that you know how big to write and how to manage the changing of pages.

Here is an idea that isn't often mentioned, but it bears examination, whenever you write on a flipchart you should always alternate the colors of the pen you use to differentiate the points on the chart. This makes

Using A Flip Chart

it easier for the audience to follow along, and creates a more visually appealing presentation.

I know some speakers are hesitant to use a white board or flipchart because they feel that their handwriting sucks. Put that idea out of your mind. The reality is you're creating a visual impact as you write and as you draw things on the chart, and that engages the audience at a different level.

Yes, it's important to try to make it as legible as possible, but you'll still win by being able to show the audiences input into your presentation no matter how pretty it is.

It's a great tool to encourage interaction, and a wonderful way to capture live and dynamic information in a presentation.

It's equally effective as a way to present information you want to talk about. It allows you to write something on the flipchart and talk about it, then come back and write something else. It brings a whole different level of personalization and customization to your presentation.

Sometimes those two things are more important than anything else in making your presentation effective.

Public Speaker Secrets

IT'S YOUR TURN...

Have you ever used a flip chart or white board during your speech? What was the reaction from the audience?

_____

_____

_____

_____

SPEAKER SECRET #31

Managing Your Notes

When it comes to notes it's a case of some do, some don't, some who do, shouldn't, and some who don't should.

In other words, it's a mixed bag. Some use notes as an excuse for standing behind a podium, and in some more formal presentations where specific data is being presented that has to be 100% accurate, that's fine.

Others use notes as a crutch and hold them in their hands as they walk around in front of the room, not realizing how much of a distraction those papers are.

Others ignore notes entirely and rely on the information that they're projecting on the screen, conveniently forgetting that this means they're often turning their back to the audience and using the screen as a crutch that leads to believing you don't need to rehearse, and therefore it compromises the presentation.

If you are using projected visuals and feel like you need them for reference, then you need to find a way to have your computer screen visible to you so that you can glance down at it without having to turn your back on the audience. But even in this case you still need to put in the rehearsal time to ensure that you're ready to deliver your message without the support of the visuals.

The simplest and easiest approach is to use a clipboard. You can simply take the clipboard and hold it in front of you, then when you need to glance down to verify information, you can do that and then come right back to your audience. It also leaves one of your hands free to gesture during your presentation.

If you don't feel like the clipboard is appropriate, you could consider using simple 3"x 5" or 5"x 7" file cards. You hold them at your side and glance at them to get the information you need and then come back to the audience.

Remember, your audiences want you to succeed. They want the information that you've come to give them. It doesn't bother them if you use notes when you present information they need to know.

The key is that you're not using notes in a way that's distracting. If you use the clipboard or the file cards, you'll find that you won't have that problem.

IT'S YOUR TURN...

Do you use notes during your presentation? How do you stop them from becoming a distraction to you and the audience?

_____

_____

_____

_____

SPEAKER SECRET #32

Using Handouts

Let me share a few tips about handouts.

There are some questions you need to address up front. First and foremost, when will you give out the handout?

Oftentimes if we give a handout at the beginning of a presentation, audience members will flip through it and jump ahead. They won't follow you.

That can be deadly in some situations.

My personal belief is that giving people a handout gives them permission to opt out of paying attention to the presentation.

Because they know they have the core content to take with them, they don't need to pay full attention, and it becomes a bit like speaking to a group of people who have something else on their minds besides listening to you.

Using Handouts

That said, few things are more important than something the audience can take with them to reinforce your message, particularly if you're trying to teach them or persuade them about something. They need that reference to go back to later, to remind them of what you said.

The idea that some quick printing, facilitated by a software program that gives the audience small images of your slides with space for notes next to them is useful to anyone is absurd.

- There's not enough space for notes
- The impact of the visual cues lose all of their impact when shrunk to a smaller size
- The small number of the audience who actually use them does not justify their preparation.

No doubt that makes it clear I'm not a big believer in the standard PowerPoint handout that some presenters use.

Few things annoy me more than a meeting planner who insists that we provide those types of ineffective handouts to the audience.

I can't tell you the number of times I've walked out of the room after bringing a large set of handouts based on the projected size of the audience, only to find half of them still lying on the table because not everyone showed up.

Public Speaker Secrets

My real point is this: people come to presentations to be informed, educated, or entertained, and only a small percentage of them take notes.

That's why I advocate having a focused summary handout that reinforces the main point you're making in your speech or presentation, and it invites the audience to learn more by listening. The handout will only reinforce points that they have heard and understood. It is not intended to give them all of the information that you're going to give them during the presentation.

PLEASE do not give people a full presentation handout during or before the presentation, save it for afterwards.

If you're giving out a reinforcement handout, that's a different thing because it essentially becomes much like a program for a play or a concert— It gives the audience a way to follow along and capture the essence of your message as you go.

Whatever your decision on handouts, always remember that you need to put your full contact information on any handout that you give to an audience, as well as, on every page of that handout.

If you do a great job and people find that your information resonates with them, they may want to contact you to have you speak to their group, so it's in your best interest to make it easy for them to do that.

One final handout tip is to make sure your handout looks professional and complete. It's not enough just to

Using Handouts

put some information on a sheet of paper and pass it out, it needs to have your branding on it, it needs to be prepared for ease of consumption, and it needs to be free of typos and grammatical errors.

Remember, handouts should be focused and used to reinforce the presentation or they should not be given out.

IT'S YOUR TURN...

When you give a presentation, do you use handouts? Why or why not?

_____

_____

_____

_____

_____

SPEAKER SECRET #33

Using Gestures

Gestures are powerful ways to illustrate key points in our presentations because most of us are quite comfortable talking with our hands.

The key to using gestures when giving a speech is to find a way to keep our hands under control.

My recommendation is simple.

Find a place where you're comfortable keeping your hands and keep them there. The exception would be when making a gesture to illustrate a specific point or reaching out to the audience and inviting them to come in with you on what you're talking about at that moment.

I know there're lots of people who have lots of rules on where your hands should go and what you should do with them during a presentation, and I personally just don't buy all that. I think it's much more important for you to be genuine and real. If you're a person who uses gestures when you talk one on one, then you should use gestures when you speak in front of the room.

I find that keeping my hands in front of me is a very comfortable position. I know others who put their hands behind them. Still others like to talk with one hand in their pocket. It's all about what puts you at ease in front of an audience.

All you're doing during your presentation is having a conversation with a group of people. As long as you don't jiggle keys or rattle the change in your pocket, who cares about where your hands are?

My best advice on this is to prepare your presentation, rehearse it several times in front of a mirror, and think about where the natural types of gestures you make fit and how they can improve and enhance the quality of presentation. Then keep rehearsing using the gestures. That will make you more comfortable with them, and that will increase the impact when you share them with an audience.

The gestures you make need to reinforce the message, not distract from it. Bring your natural and authentic self to every presentation, and your audience will love you for it.

Using Gestures

IT'S YOUR TURN...

Are you a person that talks with your hands? If not, would you be willing to learn if it enhances the effectiveness of your presentation?

_____

_____

_____

_____

SPEAKER SECRET #34

Careful Quotes Increase Impact

It's become quite popular to use quotes from famous and not-so-famous people to illustrate points in speeches.

There certainly can be power in this, but there are a couple cautions I would encourage you to consider.

- Be careful of overused quotes. There are some quotes out there that get used so often, everybody assigns different meanings to them. They essentially have become white noise.
- Use one or two quotes in a speech, not 10 or 12. A quote that positions what you talk about has power and will bring the audience in with you. Four or five quotes that you happen to like and that you think might possibly tie to your subject will tend to detract from your speech.

Careful Quotes Increase Impact

Remember, the audience came to hear you. If they wanted to hear the thoughts of people who came before you, they would read their biographies.

Your message is what matters, not how your message connects to previous messages.

When I was a college professor I opened every lecture with a quote, showed a quote during half time— yes I had a halftime in all my classes just to break up the flow, and ended each lesson with a quote that somehow reinforced the message. I believe strongly in the power of quotes when they are handled the right way.

Use quotes carefully. When you do use them, make sure to use them correctly. Nothing is worse than sitting in an audience and listening to a speaker who gives a quote you know is incorrect. It detracts from the rest of their message, and can in fact ruin their entire presentation.

And finally, put the quote on the screen and let it sit there and breathe while the audience reads it. To increase the impact, you might even consider reading it to them.

Remember that your speech is the star of the show. Any quotes you use are just supporting players.

Public Speaker Secrets

IT'S YOUR TURN...

Do you have a signature quote that you use in your presentation?

_____

_____

_____

_____

_____

SPEAKER SECRET #35

Technology Realities

We've talked about this before in terms of the need to set up and check the equipment. Let's get to the key point.

Always have a backup plan.

What will you do if you've developed a great presentation with slides you're relying on to both remind you of what you will say and reinforce your points for the audience, then the power goes out?

What if the projector bulb blows and the place where you're delivering the presentation has no backup?

Without a backup plan you, my friend, are toast.

Here are three quick ideas that will save your sanity when technology fails:

1. Make sure you've rehearsed your presentation and know it backwards and forwards.

2. Use a flipchart to share your ideas with your audience. This will make sure you stay on track and get through the information you prepared.

3. Print out your presentation and have it with you, just in case.

One other thought here, if the technology stops working don't spend too much time trying to fix it. If it looks hopeless, take control of the room and move on.

Rely on your preparation, ability, and rehearsal to push through the presentation regardless of the technical difficulties. This will give you the peace of mind to know that if the unthinkable happens, technology is not going to ruin your presentation.

Technology Realities

IT'S YOUR TURN...

Have you ever experienced a technology meltdown? What did you do to save the day?

_____

_____

_____

_____

_____

SPEAKER SECRET #36

A Caution About Microphones

Using a microphone certainly brings value in making sure you are heard by your audience, but from time to time, microphones can do strange things.

They'll emit squeals, pops, or they'll just stop working altogether.

Here are some important tips regarding microphones.

1. Decide in advance which type of microphone works best for your speaking style. Do you prefer a handheld wireless microphone or a lavalier microphone? There are pros and cons to both, but the point is to use what's best for you.

A Caution About Microphones

2. Make sure that you have fresh batteries in the microphone before you start. Any sort of wireless or handheld device that's transmitting will use up battery power fairly quickly. You want to start each presentation with brand-new batteries.

3. Make sure you know where the controls are to turn the volume up or down and how to adjust the levels. If you hear some sort of a noise, you'll need to be able to have it adjusted.

4. In the event that you can't adjust and fix it quickly, just give it up. Turn it off. Deliver your presentation by projecting your voice. If it's a huge room and that's not possible, make sure you know how to reach the technical people to get them in there as fast as you can.

5. Make sure you've pre-checked the microphone and that the sound levels have been set for your voice, not the technician's voice. I also strongly advise walking around the room while you perform this check so that you can identify the areas where weird sounds emerge because you're too close to speakers, other networks, etc.

Take these tips to heart, because the last thing you want is to have your great presentation destroyed because the technology doesn't perform properly.

Public Speaker Secrets

IT'S YOUR TURN...

What kind of steps do you take to ensure your technology performs seamlessly during your speech?

_____

_____

_____

_____

_____

SPEAKER SECRET #37

Tracking Your Stories

I had a great story planned to illustrate this next tip, but I forgot where it is.

Stories move people at an emotional level like nothing else can. Think about the best presentations you've ever heard and chances are there were stories involved.

That is, in fact, what this secret is about. Track your stories so that you always have them when you need them.

The simplest advice I can give you is to create a stories file and keep it handy at all times.

As you speak you'll accrue more and different stories, jot them down and put them in the file. Your best bet to ensure accuracy is to make sure your stories come from your experience versus those that you've simply heard about or are repeating.

Public Speaker Secrets

The next time you prepare a speech, consult the file. Pull the right stories that will work for that speech and you're ready to go.

For instance, if you're speaking to accountants, it would be a good idea to have a story in your file that relates to that audience.

You may at times want to go back to the file and add notes about what worked, what didn't, and how you can improve the story.

What you really need to have is a resource, and your stories file is that resource. Keep it handy. Build it over time, and watch the power of your presentations soar.

IT'S YOUR TURN...

Do you have a story file to use in your presentations?

_____

_____

_____

_____

_____

SPEAKER SECRET #38

Don't Be the Hero

When you use a story in a speech, be careful to not make yourself the hero.

- Don't make yourself the person who does it right when others are doing it wrong.
- Don't make yourself the person who saves the day.
- Don't make yourself the person who learns the lessons.

Why, you may ask?

Because, it's not about you.

Your audience doesn't want to hear about how awesome you are; the audience wants to hear about how awesome they are.

Ignore this lesson at your own peril.

Don't Be the Hero

We've all experienced the speaker who, in a misguided effort at validation, goes on and on about their grand exploits. They want you to love them, and you just want them to get off the stage as quickly as possible.

Even if you have to use a little editorial license, bring your audience members in. Bring someone from the organization in. Bring a historical figure in.

Make your story rely on its power alone. Don't make the audience think the speech is about you and the things you've done.

Your most effective stories will bring them in because they see themselves in it, not because they see you in it.

Remember, you are the guide, but they are Indiana Jones.

Public Speaker Secrets

IT'S YOUR TURN...

Have you ever made the mistake of making yourself the hero? How did your audience react to that?

_____

_____

_____

_____

_____

SPEAKER SECRET #39

Rehearse, Rehearse, Rehearse

I'm sure you've heard the famous line about how to get to Carnegie Hall…practice, practice, practice.

When you go out to give a speech, you want to succeed.

I want the same thing for you, and the single best tip I can give you to ensure success every time is this: rehearse, rehearse, and then rehearse some more.

The best professionals I know will arrive in a room long before they're scheduled to speak.

They feel the room out. They get a sense for where the audience will be seated in relation to the stage.

They walk the stage to figure out where they will stand as they present each of their key points.

Public Speaker Secrets

They look at the lighting and sound in the room to get a feel for how it will be to talk to that audience at that time and in that place.

They recite things to themselves that they will say in their speech, to make sure it will roll off the tongue during the speech.

That's rehearsal.

It's up to you as to how and where you do it, but I strongly urge you to rehearse every speech four, five, even six times before you ever stand up and present, especially if this is the first time you'll be giving this presentation.

Rehearsal increases the power and the impact which will result in increased confidence for you.

The absolute worst thing you can do is get on stage and "shoot from the hip." The members of your audience have paid a price to be there. Maybe they had to travel, buy a ticket, or get a babysitter just to sit in front of you and bathe in your wisdom.

Don't insult them by not being prepared.

Each time you are given the privilege to stand on a stage and speak, you are honor-bound to present your best material. That means you have to put the time in and do the hard work of preparation.

You want the recipe to having a short speaking career? Don't prepare.

Rehearse, Rehearse, Rehearse

Obviously the opposite is also true. When you speak and you've done your best to prepare, it shines through and everyone notices and appreciates it.

Do the right thing, and it will pay dividends that you can't even imagine.

Public Speaker Secrets

IT'S YOUR TURN...

Have you ever given a speech without being properly prepared? What steps did you take to make sure it never happened again?

_____

_____

_____

_____

_____

SPEAKER SECRET #40

Vocal Power

Your voice has power, and as you prepare and rehearse your speech you'll want to figure out how you'll use that power to bring your message home.

In my opinion this is the place most amateur and even many professional speakers mess up. They fail to use their voice effectively and as a result they unintentionally minimize the impact of their message.

Consider these thoughts:

- Lower your voice, become comfortable drawing back inside of yourself and speaking more softly when you want to draw people in.
- Speak just a bit louder than you think you should to emphasize a key point.
- Vary your voice to convey emotion so that the audience goes on a bit of a roller coaster ride with you through the highs and lows of the message you're sharing.

These points are especially effective when you are telling a story. If the story involves two people having a conversation, then you have the opportunity to use your voice by speaking in two different accents or in two different tones. This makes the story come alive for the audience, it engages you more deeply in the story, and it creates a much greater impact.

Varying your voice throughout your presentation, known as vocal variety, is probably the simplest thing for any speaker to accomplish.

Consider the way you converse with someone one-on-one when you're sitting over lunch:

- There are times when you're animated, energetic, and your voice is strong.
- There are times when you're being quiet, more withdrawn, and coming within yourself to share something more intimate.
- There are times when the story you're sharing requires a wide range of emotions (vocal variety).

Think of every speech you give as a one-on-one conversation. Each member of your audience receives that conversation as though it is personal between you and them, so you need to use your voice from the stage in the same way you would sitting across from them at a table or standing across from them at a meeting or reception.

Remember, your voice is your key tool. Learn to use it effectively.

Vocal Power

IT'S YOUR TURN...

Next time you are having a conversation with a friend, pay attention to how you use your voice to convey your message. Are you using the vocal variety in your presentations?

_____

_____

_____

_____

SPEAKER SECRET #41

The Power In the Pause

There is power in the pause.

When you deliver a message and want the audience to connect with the next point you make, the best way to draw them in is to pause before you make that point.

Learn to use this effectively and you can have the audience on the edge of their seats, desperate to hear what you'll say next.

Learning to pause at the right time creates emphasis, builds interest and compels your audience to pay attention.

Effective speeches have natural breaks throughout. There are moments when you make a point, and you want the audience to have some time to think about it before you continue.

We've all experienced speakers who talk too fast, try to say too much, and never take a breath. They're exhausting to listen to, and their messages are convoluted because it's hard to understand what they're trying to get across to you.

That's where the power of the pause displays its strength.

The most important place to use the pause is when you are first introduced and walk up to the platform.

Walk to the place where you'll be speaking, stand on that space while glancing out and looking into the audience. Let the power of the pause settle the room. That pause will bring people in and prepare them to hear the message you're about to deliver.

It's also important to use the pause at various times throughout your presentation for emphasis and to give the audience time to process what you just said. The pause also keeps you in charge of the room and causes the audience to become more attentive to your message.

The pause is also effective during Q&A sessions. Hearing the question, perhaps repeating it to the audience, and then pausing while you prepare to deliver your answer not only prepares the audience, it also gives you sufficient time to formulate the response and deliver it for maximum impact.

Public Speaker Secrets

Think about it…the best speeches give the audience time to engage with your message, while the worst speeches feel like a non-stop race to the end.

Get the most out of the message you've worked so hard to craft. Take full advantage of the power of the pause.

IT'S YOUR TURN...

When you deliver a presentation, does your audience have time to receive your message?

_____

_____

_____

_____

_____

SPEAKER SECRET #42

Eliminate Ums, Ahs, and Redundant Phrases

Every speaker has faced the challenge of dealing with dead air time. They feel the need to fill it with "uhms," "uhs" and "ahs."

Instead of giving a speech that has impact, they give a speech that causes distraction.

The audience is constantly counting, "How many times did he use this word or this phrase? How many "uhms" were there?"

Why does that dead air exist in the first place? It exists because you are uncomfortable with the silence. You believe that the audience will become lost somehow if you stop to take a breath.

Eliminate Ums, Ahs, and Redundant Phrases

Trust me, they won't.

If you want to get rid of this problem, there's a very simple tool you can use. That tool is a simple recording device.

Record your speech, then sit down and listen to it. Count the number of times you say "uhm," "ah" or "uh." Do the same speech again…record it again…count them again.

Do this three or four times.

You'll quickly learn to pay attention to what's causing you to say those filler words and phrases, and you'll be able to get them out of your speeches-making them far better.

This works best if you can put yourself on video, but if nothing else, pull your phone out of your pocket and record your speech over and over again until you achieve a level of mastery.

This simple tip puts you in control of your confidence, preparedness, and ultimately the effectiveness of your message.

Public Speaker Secrets

IT'S YOUR TURN...

Have you ever recorded your message? We're you happy with the first take, or did you find areas where you could improve?

_____

_____

_____

_____

_____

SPEAKER SECRET #43

Powerful Posture

Your posture has a powerful impact on your speech.

Think about it...when you present you're standing for a long period of time, often a much longer period of time than you typically would. That tends to create nervousness in your body. This causes you to do things like sway back and forth, which is terribly distracting for the audience.

Here's a simple solution for that problem.

Learn to stand on the balls of your feet, with your knees slightly bent, then face the audience in the direction you want to connect with them in that moment. If you want to go to the other side of the audience, simply turn your feet slightly but remain on the balls of your feet. Again, relax your knees slightly. This gives you freedom to move your body with the people, but it keeps you from doing the back and forth kind of thing which is distracting to them.

Public Speaker Secrets

A second important tip on posture is how to reach out to your audience...there is power in leaning forward when making key points.

Here's how you can do that and make it work effectively. Take your front foot and point it straight toward the audience. Take your back foot and put it at a right angle. That naturally brings your body forward and causes you to lean into the audience. That, in turn, compels the audience to lean into you, because they mirror what you are doing.

If you want to make the point in the other direction, you simply take the other foot, put it straight out in front of you, put the back foot at a right angle and bring your body in.

I think it's also worth noting that there are times in every speech where your posture needs to be less than perfect to illustrate something tied to what you're saying. For example, if you were telling a story in which you want the audience to feel fear, then your confident posture should change and become one that demonstrates a level of anxiety.

Keep in mind that at its heart, every speech is a performance. You are performing a role and your posture is one of the tools you use to bring your audience on a journey they will never forget.

Powerful Posture

IT'S YOUR TURN...

Have you ever caught yourself rocking back and forth on stage? Did your audience find that distracting?

_____

_____

_____

_____

_____

SPEAKER SECRET #44

Engaging Your Audience

The key for you to be effective as a presenter is to learn how to engage your audience.

There are several ways to accomplish this:

1. Simply ask them a question and ask them to raise their hand to answer.

2. You can give them a scenario. Then have them work in small groups and report their results.

3. You can ask a question and request each member of the audience to write down their thoughts.

4. Randomly sample the audience for their answers.

All of these can be effective.

Engaging Your Audience

A note of caution: When you ask the audience questions, make certain that those questions are very clear so there is no room for ambiguity. Otherwise, people get bogged down in trying to understand what it is that you want them to do.

Also, make sure that what you're asking the audience members to do is non-threatening. Ask for volunteers to share what they came up with rather than looking at specific people and saying, "What did you think?"

Don't use too many examples from the audience as it just drags out the presentation. When you ask a question, get two or three responses and then move on.

Draw all the power out of whatever it was they said and tie it to your message, but don't make the audience feel like this is a way for you to kill time, otherwise the impact disappears.

Remember, you are asking questions to connect with the audience and reinforce your message.

Public Speaker Secrets

IT'S YOUR TURN...

Do you want your message to stick with your audience? Ask relevant questions that draw them in and watch what happens.

What are the most successful ways that you use questions in your presentation?

_____

_____

_____

_____

_____

SPEAKER SECRET #45

Stage Movement

There are two schools of thought when it comes to movement on the stage during a speech. Both are derived from acting.

One says, "Find your mark. Stay on your mark. Keep your hands to your sides. Bring them up when you're gesturing, but keep them at your side when you're not."

"Don't move from the spot that you've been given on the stage. Use your head to turn to connect with the audience. Turn your body slightly. Don't move your feet."

The less traditional, more current school of thought says, "When you get ready to make a key point, reach out to the audience. Step in the general direction where you want to make that point from."

"Connect eye-to-eye with the audience. Make that point, and then return to your original place on the stage."

Obviously, I'm a fan of using movement. Movement is powerful and effective when used correctly.

The only caution here is this: Don't just move for the sake of moving.

The speaker who walks back and forth on the stage, paces or moves mindlessly side-to-side to dissipate their nervous energy does not connect well with their audience. In fact, it can become annoying for an audience.

Some people seem to be perpetual motion machines; always moving around the stage gesticulating wildly, giving no thought as to how distracting their actions are to the audience.

The real message is to tie the movement to the speech and its intent.

In some cases, it makes sense to plant yourself in the center of the stage. In other cases you want to move around and take the audience on a journey with you, allowing you to leverage the location where you're standing to connect the audience with your message.

Planning and preparing for effective stage movement reinforces the notion of getting in the room early and rehearsing so that you know where you're going to place yourself at different points of your presentation.

I've even been known to put tape on the floor to remind me of where to go during sections of the presentation based on where the chairs are and how the audience will see me at that time. This is important to consider when you're presenting in a room with pillars as they tend to block some people's line of sight.

Move as you feel comfortable, but always make sure it is planned, prepared, and rehearsed, so that your movements are not distracting and instead reinforce your message.

Public Speaker Secrets

IT'S YOUR TURN...

When you speak, do you prefer moving around the stage or standing in one place? Which do you think your audience prefers?

_____

_____

_____

_____

_____

SPEAKER SECRET #46

Record Everything

If you're committed to becoming an effective presenter, this next tip is one you will want to use.

Record every speech you give, no matter how long or short.

If it's easy to put it on video, do so because it allows you the same experience as your audience members.

If that's not convenient, simply buy a little inexpensive pocket recorder or use your smart phone. Stick it in your pocket, on the podium or on a table near where you're speaking and set it in record mode every time you talk.

Take the time to listen to those recordings. You'll hear the "uhms" and "ahs." You'll find the words and phrases that you trip over. You'll learn how your speech sounds to someone else.

I understand that for some this is a difficult thing to do. The reality is most of us don't like to hear ourselves talk because we tend to be overly critical when we listen to our own voice.

But if you want to be a successful speaker my advice is…get over it.

Be ready to take notes when listening to your recording to note the way you're using filler words to steal the breath from the air; to know where you use your voice effectively and where you don't; to capture any insight you may have regarding how the audience reacts to certain parts of the speech, and to make notes about how you would do it better next time.

Aside from hiring a professional speaking coach, this is perhaps the best possible way to becoming an effective presenter.

Record yourself every time you speak. Learn from it. Improve your presentation. Repeat the process. Each time, you'll get better and better.

IT'S YOUR TURN...

Do you record yourself when you speak? Why or why not?

_____

_____

_____

_____

SPEAKER SECRET #47

Ending Your Speech

I'd like to share a few tips that you can use to do a better job of ending your presentations and wrapping up your appearance at the location.

First, let's talk about how you close your speech. The best way is to issue a call to action.

You've given the audience a message. You've delivered it with a strong opening and some key points. Now it's time to let them know what you want them to do. You do that by telling them.

Tell them exactly what action you want them to take, invite them to take it, thank them for their time, and your speech is done.

Whether your goal was to persuade a person to take a certain action or to get them to believe a point of view, it is your responsibility to give them the next step that they need to take.

Ending Your Speech

That may be something as simple as completing a worksheet, or going to a website for more information, but they need to be guided toward your most wanted response.

It's important to note here that you only want to ask them to do one thing.

When you make more than one call to action, this creates a sense of confusion, and the confused mind never takes action.

When you ask an audience to take one action it creates an open loop in their minds. No one likes the feeling of having things left undone, so their very biology encourages them to close that loop and complete the action requested.

If you want to go the extra mile and really create the "Wow" factor with your audience, make sure the action you request them to take ties back to your message and gives them a quick win in their life.

This is the fastest way for them to stop seeing you as "just some speaker", and instead take on the coveted mantle of "trusted advisor".

Remember, ask them to take one action that ties back to your message and benefits them…this is the fast track to speaking success.

Public Speaker Secrets

IT'S YOUR TURN...

Do you issue a call to action at the end of your presentation?

_____

_____

_____

_____

_____

SPEAKER SECRET #48

Always End On Time

This may be the most important tip I have given you… always end on time.

If you were hired to make a 30-minute presentation, it's your mandate to wrap up and be finished on time (or better yet slightly before). If you get started late you still need to finish on schedule, don't presume that it's alright to take up another speaker's time because someone took yours.

There are two reasons for this:

1. The first is that the audience will have seen the published end time. They'll stop paying attention about five minutes in advance of the end because they'll expect you to be wrapping up.
2. The more important reason is that the person who invited you to give the speech is depending on you to keep them on schedule. If you want to be invited back, stay on schedule.

Public Speaker Secrets

In my decade as a college professor, there was one thing I learned right away. Those students knew when class was scheduled to end, and you better believe that they were going to leave on time...whether I was finished or not.

That doesn't change once you leave school.

As a professional speaker, I've gone over-time, I've ended on time, and I've ended ahead of schedule. The responses from audiences have been exactly as you would expect.

When I've gone over, multiple people have complained. When I've ended on time, some have seemed slightly annoyed, but when I've ended ahead of schedule I've received the gratitude of the audience, and I'm usually invited back to speak again.

If you are forced to cut your presentation short, I would recommend letting the audience know there are other points to cover, and you'll be sticking around after the speech to answer any questions. The best part is that those who really want the information will seek you out, and perhaps lead to new business.

Treat your audience the way you would like to be treated. Be aware of their needs, and let the ones who resonated with your message find you.

IT'S YOUR TURN...

Do you have a Plan B in case you need to cut your presentation short?

_____

_____

_____

_____

_____

SPEAKER SECRET #49

Close With Impact

Have you ever been sitting in a presentation, and because of the speaker's method of delivery you never really know when they're done speaking?

Awkward.

I have a surefire way to ensure that never happens to you.

Ask the same person who introduced you to be the one who helps you close out the speech with impact by starting the applause when you bring your speech to a conclusion.

For example: You've issued your call to action, you've looked at the audience and thanked them by gently bowing your head. At that moment, your initiator in the audience should rise and begin the applause. That makes the audience comfortable because they know you're

Close With Impact

finished, they know they're supposed to join that person in applause.

As the applause comes to an end, you simply turn to whoever is in charge of the meeting and say, "It was a pleasure being here. I'd like to turn the meeting back over to you".

I understand that this isn't practical in every situation, but where you can use it, you should.

Everyone wins.

The person who hired you is assured of a rousing ovation for you, the potential awkward moment is avoided, and you feel great receiving the adulation due you for your timely message.

Public Speaker Secrets

IT'S YOUR TURN...

What steps do you take to avoid awkward moments in your presentation?

_____

_____

_____

_____

_____

SPEAKER SECRET #50

Thank People Properly

Thanking the audience is very important. You also want to thank the person who introduced you, the person who invited you, and so forth.

However, avoid thanking these people at the start of your presentation. You need that time to open your message with impact.

After you have closed, after your "friend" in the audience has started the applause, and after the applause has died down, simply say, "I'd like to thank so-and-so for inviting me, so-and-so for introducing me and all of you for your time and attention."

Don't make the mistake of discounting the value of your message with a simple thank you.

If you've done your job and delivered a great presentation, the audience will thank you with their applause. You can then take the time to thank them when they finish that process.

Public Speaker Secrets

Some might argue that the tip I'm sharing here is irrelevant in today's fast-paced world, but I would strongly disagree. You want to make sure you thank the audience before they go racing out of the room.

Another thing I would add here is the importance of following up promptly after the event with either a hand written personal note to the key people who have helped make your presentation a success, or with an email, a phone call, or whatever is appropriate.

If you ever want to be invited back, this is a sure way to make sure that happens. You'll stand out from the crowd, you'll differentiate yourself in the way you do business, and you'll make much stronger connections.

It's worth every second that it takes.

Thank People Properly

IT'S YOUR TURN...

How do you show your appreciation to the audience at the conclusion of your presentation?

_____

_____

_____

_____

SPEAKER SECRET #51

Handling the Q&A

For some speakers, answering questions may be the most difficult part of their presentation.

There will be people in the audience who see this as a chance to show that they know more than you. Sometimes they'll even interrupt you in the middle of your speech with a difficult question.

Then there are the ones who turn their question into an hour-long presentation by itself. They tell you all about their backstory and do a deep dive into the meaning of their earth shattering question.

Of course, there are those who desire to ask a question, but just can't put enough cohesive thoughts together to make any sense.

Handling the Q&A

Here are my best tips on running a successful Q&A session:

- When a question is asked in the middle of your speech, before you answer it, simply say, "I'd like to come back to that question and answer it later. Would that be okay with you?" There are very few people who won't give you that control and say, "Yes, that's fine." Be sure to make a note of the question or have someone in the audience do that. Come back to it at the appropriate time.

- Always repeat the question before answering it. This allows you time to make sure you really understand the question as it was asked, it gives you time to formulate an answer, and it lets everyone in the audience hear the question you are answering.

Let's suppose someone asks you a question and you don't know the answer. What do you say? "I don't know" is a perfectly acceptable answer if you truly don't know. You may want to say, "I don't know. I'd like to get some more information about that and get back to you. Give me your card after the presentation and I'll make sure I get back to you."

You may also face a situation where you get into a very good conversation with an individual member of the audience, but it's going further than you want it to go and it's starting to distract the audience from your message.

In those cases, simply look at the person and say, "Could we talk about this at the break? I'm really interested, but I sense that there are some other questions in the room. I want to make sure that we get to those."

Here is one final tip on questions. If you can learn how to do this, it will be amazingly powerful for you.

Always answer by giving three alternatives.

Most of the world isn't black and white. When someone asks a question, oftentimes they have an answer that they believe is correct. They're checking to see if your thinking matches theirs.

If you learn to give three alternatives to most questions, you'll bring the audience along. You give them a black-and-white viewpoint as well as a grey viewpoint in the middle.

When the question is asked, you simply set it up and say, "Well, there are three ways you could look at that. First you could see this," and provide Point A. "Then you could see this," and provide Point B. Then create a third alternative that fits between the other two.

That way, everyone in the audience can see how your thinking connects with theirs, and you'll create a higher level of understanding with the people you're talking with.

Another option is to provide each audience member with a card with which they can submit their questions. This way you won't be blindsided by an awkward question, and if they leave their contact information you can follow-up at a later time. As a side note, this can also lead to new business.

If handled correctly, the Q&A is a magnificent opportunity to connect with your audience, present a clearer picture of your message, and position yourself as an authority on your subject.

Public Speaker Secrets

IT'S YOUR TURN...

What are your best practices for a Q&A session?

_____

_____

_____

_____

_____

SPEAKER SECRET #52

Always Leave Late

Our last Speaker Secret for closing your presentation is this: Always leave late.

You are the speaker. You are the focus of the meeting. Your presentation is why people came. The last thing they want to see is you running out the door when they had a question they wanted to ask you at the next break.

Plan your schedule so that you have time to linger in the room a bit, to talk to the people who want to pursue the subject you've shared and interact with those who want more information.

Many speakers drop the ball here. There's an old statement with regard to speakers that "blow in, blow off, and blow out." This is not the person you want to be. Granted, sometimes travel schedules may force you to leave quickly, but in general try to book your travel so you have at least enough time to spend with the audience until they enter their next session or event.

Public Speaker Secrets

Even better, in some cases you should schedule yourself to be with the audience for the remainder of the day if possible. This will give you a chance to make stronger connections and grow your business more effectively, as well as an opportunity to see how your message was actually received. This can help you tailor your presentation for maximum effectiveness next time.

More than anything, this shows the audience that you respect their time and that you came for them.

IT'S YOUR TURN...

What steps do you take to add value for your audience after your presentation?

_____

_____

_____

_____

_____

ABOUT THE AUTHOR

Dr. Michael Hudson is a teacher, speaker, writer, facilitator, coach, & ideapreneur. He works with speakers, coaches, & consultants, entrepreneurs & small business owners, and leaders of cause-focused organizations seeking to get clear on their message and to communicate it to create their impact on the world.

A former tenured professor at both the University of Illinois and Cornell University, Michael has served as a trusted advisor to over 3,000 growing businesses, government agencies, and non-profit organizations, helping them define and implement strategies for growth, develop their leaders, clarify, and communicate their message.

Michael has delivered over 8,000 paid presentations across the past 31 years. He leverages the lessons learned from those experiences to teach his coaching clients an audience-centered approach that helps them grow their businesses and increase their impact.

About The Author

As one who grew up fearing public speaking, Michael is committed to helping people develop their abilities to communicate their messages to those who need to hear it. He regularly speaks at conferences and conventions sharing his personal story—revealing the power of personal experience to lead the audience to take action.

For more resources, and to subscribe to Michael's free e-mail newsletter, visit MichaelHudson.com.

HOW TO CONTACT MICHAEL

If you are interested in clarifying and communicating your message to increase your impact, using speaking to grow your business, or becoming a better speaker, Michael can help.

For more information about keynotes, workshops, facilitated events, and coaching services, contact Big Idea Guru, LLC:

Phone: (302) 242-7038

Email: info@michaelhudson.com

Online: www.MichaelHudson.com

Big Idea Guru, LLC
18766 John J Williams Hwy
Unit 4, #387, Rehoboth Beach, DE 19971

Sign up for Michael's email newsletter at:
www.MichaelHudson.com

www.ingramcontent.com/pod-product-compliance
Lightning Source LLC
Chambersburg PA
CBHW070317190526
45169CB00005B/1659